CONTENTS

TORNADOES

ANN ARMBRUSTER
AND ELIZABETH A. TAYLOR

Franklin Watts
New York/London/Toronto/Sydney
A First Book/1989

TORNADOES

The evolution of a tornado is traced through the sequence of ten photos that appear in this space throughout the book.

The tornado occurred near Denver, Colorado, on July 2, 1987 and was photographed by Roger Wakimoto of the NCAR.

Cover photo courtesy of NOAA

Illustrations by Joe LeMonnier

Photographs courtesy of:
NCAR: pp. 22 (Roger Wakimoto), 26 (bottom, NFS), 41; NOAA: pp. 6 (top, Joe Golden), 17, 18 (top), 26 (top), 30 (top left, Joe Golden), 30 (top right and bottom left), 37, 45, 50, 52; Bettmann Archive: pp. 6 (bottom), 9; Photo Researchers: pp. 11 (R.F. Head/National Audubon Society), 18 (bottom, Howie Bluestein), 30 (bottom right, Roger Appleton), 60 (Lawrence Migdale); UNISIS Corp.: p. 44.

Library of Congress Cataloging-in-Publication Data

Armbruster, Ann.
Tornadoes / by Ann Armbruster and Elizabeth A. Taylor.
p. cm.—(A First book)
Bibliography: p.
Includes index.
Summary: Describes the causes, different parts, and movements of tornadoes, discusses how they are tracked and studied by scientists, and suggests science projects and related activities.
ISBN 0-531-10755-8
1. Tornadoes—Juvenile literature. [1. Tornadoes.] I. Taylor, Elizabeth A. II. Title. III. Series.
QC955.A76 1989
551.55'3—dc20 89-31827 CIP AC

INTRODUCTION

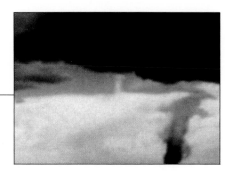

From the far north they heard a low wail of the wind, and Uncle Henry and Dorothy could see where the long grass bowed in waves before the coming storm. There now came a sharp whistling in the air from the south and as they turned their eyes that way they saw ripples in the grass coming from that direction also. Suddenly Uncle Henry stood up. "There's a cyclone coming, Em," he called to his wife: "I'll go look after the stock." Aunt Em dropped her work and came to the door. One glance told her of the danger close at hand. "Quick, Dorothy," she screamed, "run for the cellar."

This scene from *The Wizard of Oz* describes the adventures of Dorothy, a young Kansas farm girl carried away by a cyclone to the fabulous land of Oz. Although the book is a fantasy, cyclones are not fantasies to the inhabitants of Kansas, Oklahoma, and other sections of the United States where people and objects in the path of a tornado can be suddenly swept up and deposited somewhere else.

People in tornado areas often use an underground cellar or cave for protection from the storm. When tornado sirens sound, people without basements will head to the nearest storm cellar, where they may keep blankets, bottled water, transistor radios, and first-aid supplies.

HOW TORNADOES FORM

A tornado is commonly called a *cyclone* in the Midwest. Perhaps you have seen miniature tornadoes over a hot pavement, swirling the dust and scraps of paper around and around, higher and higher. Cool air from a nearby shady wall flows along the ground toward the hot pavement, pushing up the heated air.

Big tornadoes are made in much the same way. They start when cold, dry air coming from a westerly direction catches up with unusually warm, moist air from the south. The resulting whirlwind is accompanied by thick, black clouds and thunderstorms. When a gust of warm air rises with a spiraling motion, water vapor is swept upward. In cooling, it forms a twisting, funnel-shaped cloud. This cloud, called a *vortex* but often referred to as an elephant's trunk, is the trademark of the tornado.

Cold air lashes around the outside of the funnel, causing a roar that can be heard for miles. An upward draft within the funnel lowers the pressure in the funnel's center as the tornado sweeps over an area. Dust, pebbles, water—anything in the tornado's path—are whirled upward. The tornado travels as it spins, smashing and destroying until all the heated air that was near land has been squeezed up by the cooler, heavier, inflowing air. When there is no more warm air to be pushed up, the air stops flowing, and the tornado dies.

For the early Greeks, Aeolus—keeper or god of the winds—was believed to be responsible for storms, hurricanes and other wild weather.

THE MYTHOLOGY OF WIND

Since ancient times, humankind has been searching for explanations for the wind. The early Greek god Aeolus was thought to be in charge of all winds. He kept them locked in a cave with eight openings, each blocked by a large rock. Occasionally, he would roll one of the rocks away, creating frost, moderate winds, or full-blown hurricanes, all according to his whim.

Today in Greece there stands a structure called the Tower of the Winds, built before the time of Christ. The forerunner of today's weather station, it has eight sides and is about 32 feet (10 m) in height and 26 feet (8.6 m) around. Each side shows a figure representing a different wind. Boreas

(BOH-ree-as) was the rough north wind. Our word *boreal*, which means north, comes from this.

In another myth, Wind is captured and is about to be killed when it craftily bargains for its release by promising to blow only four times in the future. Among the Eastern Woodland Indians, heroes could successfully control the wind. These beliefs were not unlike those of the ancient Greeks.

In Scotland, witches used to raise the wind by dipping a rag in water and beating it on a stone three times, saying:

> *I knock this rag upon the stone*
> *To raise the wind in the devil's name.*
> *It shall not lie till I please again.*

The Greek writer Aristotle seems to have anticipated the modern idea of a polar front. He divided the winds into two classes—polar and equatorial—and described with amazing accuracy the weather likely to be brought by each.

In the United States, the first written description of a tornado was made by colonist Ralph Lane. Spotting some waterspouts (tornadoes over water) at sea, he wrote that "we had thunder and rain with hailstones as big as hen's eggs. There were great spouts at the seas as though heaven and earth would have me." Benjamin Franklin also gathered information on winds. He noted that, contrary to the accepted belief, wind moves from west to east. He published his observations in *Poor Richard's Almanack* for the benefit of farmers and sailors.

A fascinating early device invented to change the wind was the "cyclone destroyer" of John B. Atwater, patented in 1886. Explosives were supposed to interrupt the force of the winds.

TORNADO FACT SHEET

A tornado is a small, intense storm.

About six hundred to seven hundred tornadoes are reported in the United States each year.

People in some regions call a tornado a "twister" or a "cyclone."

Their damage paths are generally a few hundred feet wide and a few miles long.

Tornadoes can occur at any time of the year but are most likely to happen in spring and summer.

The word *tornado* is derived from the Spanish word *tronada*, which means "thunderstorm."

Tornadoes occur mostly in the United States.

Texas holds the record for the greatest number of tornadoes.

A tornado over water is called a *waterspout*.

Twisting down to the surface of the sea on the left is a waterspout; to the right, another is beginning to form.

No one really knows exactly how the noise of a tornado is produced.

About one out of every four tornadoes comes between 4 P.M. and 6 P.M.

The force of a tornado has been known to drive straws right through boards.

Tornadoes have lifted frogs and fish from ponds, then dropped them over populated areas, thus the saying, "a tornado may rain frogs."

A storm cellar or basement is a good place to go during a tornado.

Many tornadoes can develop over a fairly large area.

Tornadoes can now be detected with weather radar.

Tornado watches and warnings save many lives annually.

1

CONDITIONS ARE RIGHT

Have you ever taken part in a tornado drill at school? If you live in one of four states (Kansas, Missouri, Oklahoma, or Texas), you have. These states, sometimes called *tornado alley*, lie in the path of most of the tornadoes that develop in the United States.

You might be surprised to know that most of the tornadoes in the world form in the midwestern United States. Conditions there during the spring and early summer are just right for these violent storms to develop. The greatest number of U.S. tornadoes (about 75 percent) occur between March and July. Records show that April tornadoes have caused the greatest number of deaths. What is it about the Midwest during these months that allows the formation of so many deadly storms?

Look at Figure 1. The blue arrow shows the path of the cool, dry air, which moves eastward from the Rocky Mountains. This air is part of an air mass that moves southward from the polar regions. The red arrow shows the path of warm, moist air moving into the same region from the Gulf of Mexico and the Caribbean Sea. As warm weather returns to the North American continent in the spring, the path of

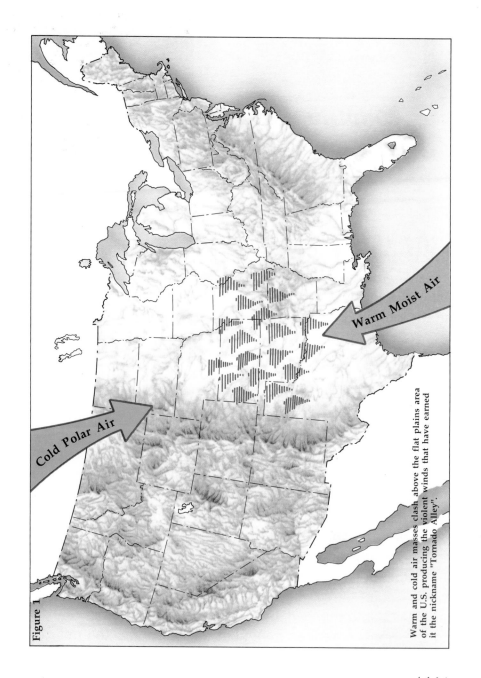

Figure 1

Cold Polar Air

Warm Moist Air

Warm and cold air masses clash above the flat plains area of the U.S. producing the violent winds that have earned it the nickname "Tornado Alley".

this warm air flow moves farther north with each passing month. The strongest storms form when the temperature differences between air masses are the greatest.

Warm, moist air is lighter than cool, dry air at the same pressure. Because the cool air is heavy, we say that it is *high pressure* air. We say that the warm air is *low pressure* air because it is lighter and doesn't press down on the earth with as much force.

The boundary between the cool upper air layer and the warm lower air layer may be a thin stream of air called a *capping inversion.* As time passes during the day, the ground will be warmed by the sun. The air above the ground will absorb some of this heat and may also pick up moisture from evaporation. If the capping inversion breaks down at one or more points, the warm, moist air below will burst upward. Figure 2 shows these layers.

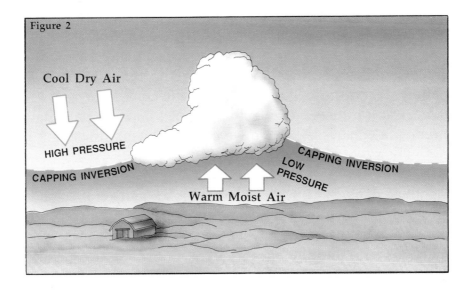

Figure 2

Cool Dry Air

HIGH PRESSURE

CAPPING INVERSION

CAPPING INVERSION

LOW PRESSURE

Warm Moist Air

CLOUD FORMATION

Moisture contained in the warmer, lower air condenses as it rises. The water droplets that condense out of the warm air settle on dust particles in the air and become clouds. At first, the clouds may be fluffy-looking, white, cumulus clouds. But later, they may become the dark cumulonimbus clouds that many people call thunderheads.

Thunderheads are dark because they are so tall (sometimes as tall as 10 miles, or 16 km) that they block out the sun's light. When you look at thunderheads, you can see the clouds in them rolling about, almost as if they were boiling in a pot.

LIGHTNING

Thunderheads usually bring thunderstorms with them. The water droplets in the cloud collect to form water drops. The drops fall to the earth as rain. At the same time, electricity builds up within the clouds. Some parts of the cloud are positively charged (+) and some parts are negatively charged (−). These charges move about and eventually separate. The cloud then becomes a kind of electric cell, similar to a battery. When the buildup of charges becomes very great, there is a discharge of electricity that follows a path between the positive and negative charges within the cloud.

OTHER DANGERS

Lightning bolts can travel within the cloud, move from cloud to cloud, or move from the cloud to the ground. As you can imagine, all this electricity flashing around releases tremendous heat into the air. As the air is heated, it expands with a violent rush. The sound of this rapidly moving air is

*A fluffy-looking white cumulus cloud (top) may become
dense, with a dark base from which rain may begin to fall.
It is then called a cumulonimbus (bottom).*

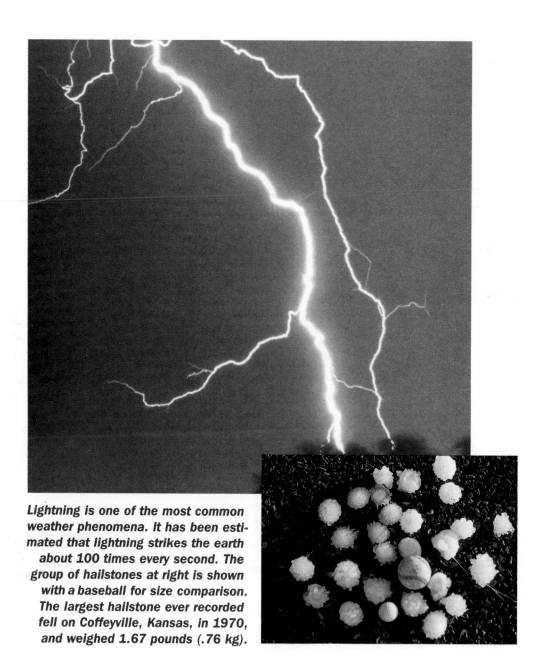

Lightning is one of the most common weather phenomena. It has been estimated that lightning strikes the earth about 100 times every second. The group of hailstones at right is shown with a baseball for size comparison. The largest hailstone ever recorded fell on Coffeyville, Kansas, in 1970, and weighed 1.67 pounds (.76 kg).

called *thunder*. Thunder will usually sound like a sharp crack if lightning is close by or a rumble if it is farther away.

Thunderstorms frequently occur without tornadoes following them. But tornadoes do not occur unless a thunderstorm happens first. During a thunderstorm there is danger from:

> *Lightning* (Be sure you seek shelter.)

> *Rain* (Flashfloods can result in death. Be careful where you seek shelter.)

> *Winds* (Even if a tornado does not develop, high winds can cause damage or death.)

> *Hail* (Hail isn't usually deadly but can still damage property.)

Hailstones are evidence that a tornado may be on the way. Hailstones form when powerful, upward-moving gusts of air (called *updrafts*) carry raindrops to higher, colder air layers, where they are frozen. As these ice pellets drop back toward the earth, they may pick up a layer of moisture and be carried upward again and again. With each upward journey the hailstones get bigger, until they are too heavy to remain aloft. If you count the rings in a hailstone, you can tell how many times it has been carried by updrafts. See Figure 3.

Hailstones are studied by scientists interested in predicting tornadoes. The size of a hailstone indicates the intensity of a thunderstorm.

You might be wondering what hailstones could tell scientists about tornado formation. Tornadoes are dangerous storms because of the high winds they produce. These winds

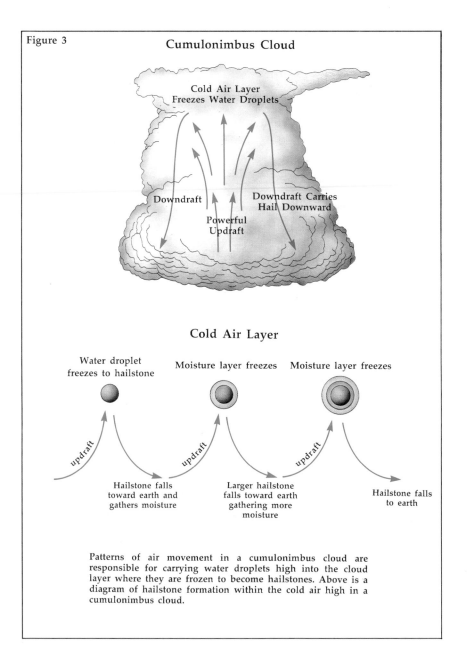

Figure 3

Cumulonimbus Cloud

Cold Air Layer
Freezes Water Droplets

Downdraft

Downdraft Carries
Hail Downward

Powerful
Updraft

Cold Air Layer

Water droplet
freezes to hailstone

Moisture layer freezes

Moisture layer freezes

updraft

updraft

updraft

Hailstone falls
toward earth and
gathers moisture

Larger hailstone
falls toward earth
gathering more
moisture

Hailstone falls
to earth

Patterns of air movement in a cumulonimbus cloud are responsible for carrying water droplets high into the cloud layer where they are frozen to become hailstones. Above is a diagram of hailstone formation within the cold air high in a cumulonimbus cloud.

are caused by the great differences in air pressure and temperature that produce hail. Hail warns us that conditions may be right for a tornado to develop.

A TORNADO IS BORN

Throughout tornado season, weather conditions that can produce a tornado occur many times. What exactly takes place to turn the possibility of a tornado's occurrence into a certainty?

The first factor is a strong thunderstorm. During a powerful thunderstorm, there are constant updrafts. These result in a rising stream of very low-pressure air. Like a vacuum cleaner, the stream of air draws surrounding air from the ground upward and toward it.

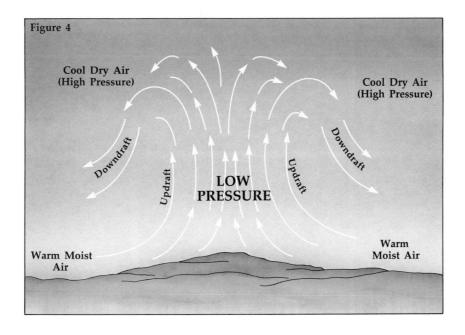

Figure 4

Cool Dry Air
(High Pressure)

Cool Dry Air
(High Pressure)

Downdraft

Downdraft

Updraft

Updraft

LOW
PRESSURE

Warm Moist
Air

Warm
Moist Air

This series of photographs shows the formation of a tornado. The cloud evolves from a small cumulus to a very dense and well-developed cumulonimbus. The tornado is then spawned from the cumulonimbus base.

As warm, upward-moving air cools, precipitation forms. Where precipitation begins to fall, powerful downdrafts are created. One downdraft usually forms on the northeast side of the updraft and another on the southwest side. Each updraft-downdraft pair in a thunderstorm is called a *cell*. Many cells may form in one thunderstorm. Each cell usually has a life of about thirty minutes. As a thunderstorm moves, new cells form and old ones die. A *supercell* develops when all the individual cells in a storm work together. The result is a violent, rotating storm. The tornado is most likely to develop along the line where the southwest downdraft meets the updraft. See Figure 4.

More and more ground-level air is drawn into the updraft. Thus, the low-pressure column is fed, and the updraft is strengthened. As powerful as the updraft is, it can't be classified as a tornado unless it begins to rotate (spin). An important factor influencing the rotation of air is the *Coriolis effect*.

Because the earth rotates on its axis, we experience cycles of daylight and darkness. We also experience planetary wind patterns.

Figure 5 shows that winds curve from east to west in the Northern Hemisphere near the equator. This air flow is in the opposite direction to the earth's spin and is called the Coriolis effect.

Because the earth spins on its axis, it is constantly moving under its atmosphere, causing the air to turn aside. To understand how this happens, imagine yourself standing on the earth's surface (see Figure 6).

Warm air at the equator rises and moves toward the North and South poles. On its journey toward the North Pole,

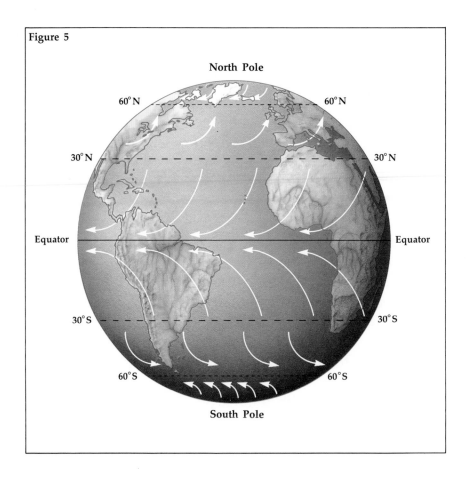

Figure 5

North Pole

60° N   60° N

30° N   30° N

Equator   Equator

30° S   30° S

60° S   60° S

South Pole

the air cools and begins to sink to the earth's surface. When it has completed about one-third of its journey, it splits into two streams. One stream flows south and bends to the right, becoming the Easterlies. The other continues northward and bends to the left, becoming the Westerlies.

The Westerlies stream across the United States, turning the air into giant pinwheels as they go. These pin-

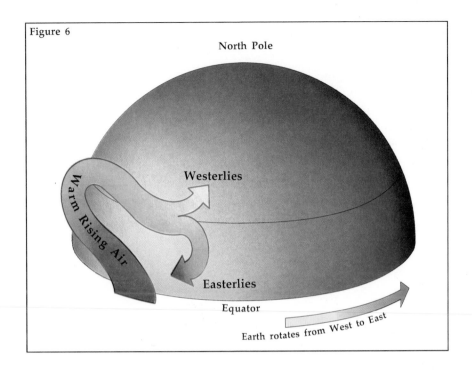

Figure 6

North Pole

Westerlies

Warm Rising Air

Easterlies

Equator

Earth rotates from West to East

wheels, called high- and low-pressure areas, can be seen on a weather map.

Remember that a low-pressure system appears before a thunderstorm develops. The lower the pressure, the more violent the resulting storm, and the greater the storm's speed of rotation. Rotation begins at a height of about 2 to 4 miles (3.2 to 6.4 km) above the earth's surface. Strong winds blowing in a straight line force the air ahead of it to roll into a tubelike shape. When a powerful updraft strikes the tube, it is tilted upright, like a giant smokestack. The air in the tube is forced to spin in a counterclockwise direction by the Coriolis effect.

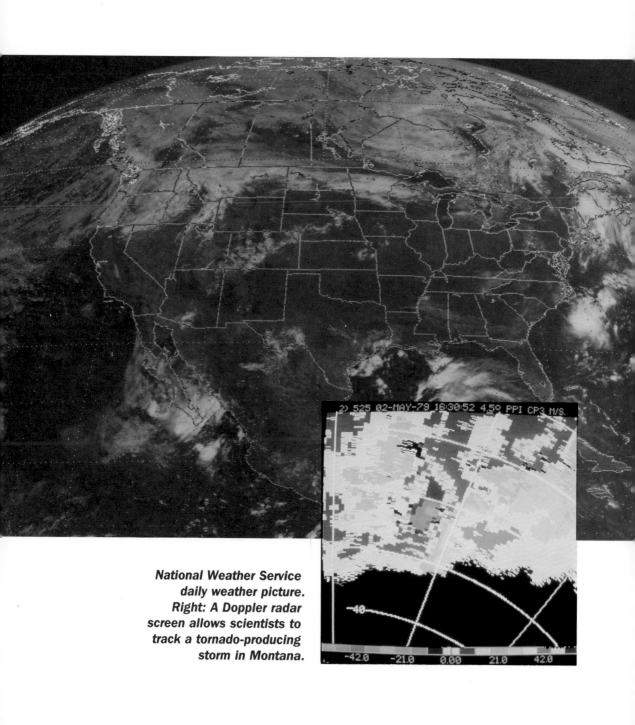

2) 525 02-MAY-79 16:30:52 4.5º PPI CP3 M/S.

-40

-42.0   -21.0   0.00   21.0   42.0

National Weather Service daily weather picture. Right: A Doppler radar screen allows scientists to track a tornado-producing storm in Montana.

Two conditions cause the swirling tube to spin faster. The pressure in the tube drops significantly. This causes an inward pulling force. An outward pull is generated by the tube's rotation. These two conditions cause the sides of the tube to be sealed off. No air can be sucked in through the sides. Air has to be sucked in from the bottom of the tube (the end nearest the ground). Since all the air enters from ground level, the updraft becomes even stronger, and the tube spins faster still. As the process continues, the speed of the wind decreases the tube's diameter. The column of air is narrowed and stretches itself downward.

Is this swiftly spinning tube of air a tornado? Not yet. At this point, the spiraling tube is about 1 to 3 miles (1.6 to 4.8 km) in diameter. We do not yet understand why, but a small vortex may begin to develop inside the larger tube. The small vortex is usually no more than a quarter to a half-mile in diameter and is located near one wall of the larger tube.

Scientists using a special kind of radar called *Doppler radar* have observed that this new vortex begins above the ground and stretches downward just as the larger tube does. The newly formed vortex is able to spin much faster than the larger tube and reaches very close to the ground. The greatest wind speeds in the vortex are at the base of the spiral, which is now called a *funnel cloud.*

2

ANATOMY OF A TORNADO

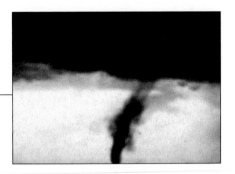

Many clouds have a threatening appearance. However, the best way to tell if a tornado is forming is to look for a steady, consistent rotation at the base of a cumulonimbus cloud. It is in this region that a funnel develops. The rotation need not be rapid, but it must be continuous.

The funnel that forms can be seen extending from the lower part of its mother cloud toward the ground. Witnesses have reported seeing funnels emerge, then draw back into the cloud.

As the funnel descends, it may whip about wildly or wave gracefully. Some funnels lower themselves to the ground in the shape of a thread or a rope. Some look like ice cream cones; others form columns so broad they look like walls.

When the funnel descends from the mother cloud, it is usually white in color. Some funnels appear to shimmer. Strong updrafts cause water vapor inside the funnel to condense, darkening it.

When the funnel strikes the ground, friction causes it to curve. Dust and debris from the ground begin to churn and scatter. Light reflecting from dust and other ground debris often gives the vortex a greenish glow. The rain accompanying the twister lifts and scatters more loose material, causing the vortex to darken even more and appear more solid.

PATH OF THE TORNADO

Once the funnel touches the ground, it may move in either a straight line or a series of loops. The vortex may stand still for a number of seconds, or it may reverse its direction and retrace its own path. Some vortices have been known to hop over objects on the ground before resuming their destruction.

Even if there are no witnesses, a tornado's path can be determined by the tracks it leaves behind. Most tracks show that tornadoes travel from southwest to northeast. But, as is usual with tornadoes, there are exceptions. Some tornadoes move from north to south.

Tornadoes can produce several funnels. The paths these funnels take are especially unpredictable; each funnel in the group can move in a different direction. Multiple-funnel tornadoes are the most dangerous, partly for this reason. Tornado spotters have tracked storms for several hours, observing them change from single to multiple funnels. Such a storm struck Friendship, Oklahoma, on May 11, 1982, killing one person. Warnings and prompt action by citizens kept the death toll from going higher.

Whether funnels move in a straight line or in a twisted path, the forward movement of the tornado along the ground is very fast. Much faster still is the movement of air within the tornado's spiral.

As it travels, the funnel's forward speed is the same as the speed of its mother cloud. Speeds can range from 30

A tornado's funnel-shaped cloud may take different forms.

to 70 miles per hour (48 to 166 kmph). Because of the high speed, people are advised not to try outrunning a tornado even in a very fast car.

WIND SPEEDS

The winds that compose the vortex may blow at speeds up to 350 mph (560 kmph). It has been suggested that the roaring noises produced by a tornado are the sounds of spiraling winds breaking the sound barrier, thus producing a sonic boom. Although meteorologists have calculated speeds of 150 mph (240 kmph), it is impossible to measure wind speed in the vortex because anemometers (instruments that measure wind speed) break apart under tornado winds.

The measurement of wind speeds within the vortex is further complicated because the funnel is moving along the ground. The right side of the tornado moves faster than the left side. The speed of the funnel's forward movement must be added to the speed of rotation on the funnel's right side. It must be subtracted from the speed of rotation on the funnel's left side.

For example, the funnel in Figure 7 is moving along with its mother cloud at 50 mph (80 kmph). This set of conditions means that winds in the funnel's right side roar along at 170 mph (272 kmph), while those on the left side carry a force of 70 mph (112 kmph). A house on the right side of this tornado will be hit with a wind force 100 mph (161 kmph) greater than a house hit by the left side.

In tornadoes that produce several funnels, calculating the speed can become even more complicated. These multiple-vortex tornadoes produce several funnels that all rotate about a central point in the cumulonimbus cloud.

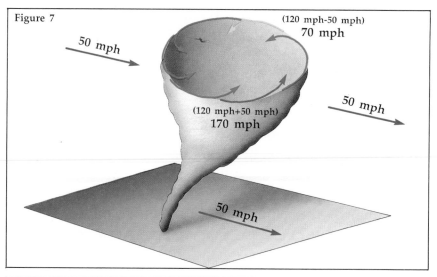

Figure 7

50 mph

(120 mph-50 mph)
70 mph

(120 mph+50 mph)
170 mph

50 mph

50 mph

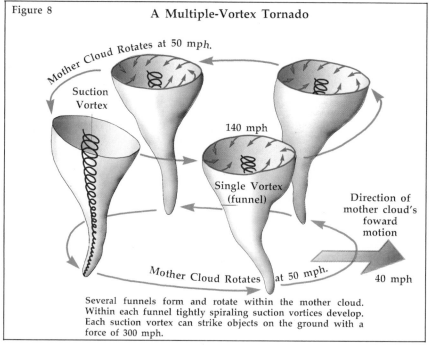

Figure 8

A Multiple-Vortex Tornado

Mother Cloud Rotates at 50 mph.

Suction
Vortex

140 mph

Single Vortex
(funnel)

Direction of
mother cloud's
foward
motion

40 mph

Mother Cloud Rotates at 50 mph.

Several funnels form and rotate within the mother cloud.
Within each funnel tightly spiraling suction vortices develop.
Each suction vortex can strike objects on the ground with a
force of 300 mph.

The speed of each funnel in a multiple-vortex tornado is calculated by adding the speed of the mother cloud's forward movement, the speed of the revolution (movement around the mother cloud's center in a circular path) of one vortex, and the rotation speed of that same vortex. A funnel cloud (see Figure 8) whose mother cloud advances at 40 mph (64 kmph), revolves with the cloud at 50 mph (80 kmph), has vortex winds that rotate at 140 mph (224 kmph), and can strike with a total force of 230 mph (368 kmph).

RATING A TORNADO

Meteorologists use a certain scale to rate the intensity of tornadoes. This scale is based on the wind speeds that tornadoes generate. It is called the *Fujita-Pearson Tornado Intensity Scale,* after the two men who developed it: Dr. Theodore Fujita of the University of Chicago and Allan Pearson, head of the Forecast Center in Kansas City.

The Fujita-Pearson Tornado Intensity Scale

Classification	Wind Speed	Damage
F0	72 MPH	Light
F1	73–112 MPH	Moderate
F2	113–157 MPH	Considerable
F3	158–206 MPH	Severe
F4	207–260 MPH	Devastating
F5	260 MPH	Unbelievable

PRESSURE CHANGES

As we have seen, wind speeds vary within the mother cloud's area of rotation. It is now believed that the force of the winds within the funnel is responsible for the great damage done by tornadoes. In the past, many meteorologists thought that the great drop in pressure caused air in the buildings to expand and explode. This explosive force was thought to be the most destructive power in the storm.

By studying the wreckage left behind after a tornado, scientists discovered a pattern in the scattered debris. Most of the debris falls on the windward side of the funnel (the side from which a tornado approaches). If the differences in pressure were responsible for the damage, the fragments would be found on the leeward side (the side opposite the one hit by the tornado).

Survivors have reported feeling the pressure change as a tornado's eye has passed them overhead. Some have reported mild sensations such as a popping in their ears, while others have experienced more severe reactions, such as light-headedness and difficulty in breathing.

An interview appearing in Dennis Fradin's book *Disaster! Tornado* quotes one survivor, Imogene Hall, as saying, "My ears were stopped up and it felt like my head would explode outward." Another survivor, Dennis Spruill, said, "I could feel the tornado pulling my hair and my clothes upward. I could feel it tugging on me . . . I felt that the tornado was about to suck me out of the room."

LIGHTNING

Another phenomenon observed during tornadoes is lightning. Flashes of lightning are commonly reported by those who have been close enough to the funnel to give a good description. The sharp odor of ozone associated with lightning is usual, and hissing and crackling sounds can be heard. Static builds up on radios and television sets as the storm approaches; sometimes, the bursts of static are so close together that a tornado is easy to distinguish from an ordinary thunderstorm. Bernard Vonnegut, a prominent weather scientist, has suggested that electrical activity in a powerful thunderstorm might actually help to start the tornado, and that this same electrical energy may add fuel to the tornado and lengthen its life.

PARTS OF A TORNADO'S THUNDERSTORM

In a tornado's thunderstorm, many activities go on at the same time. The diagram shows you the parts of a tornado-producing storm.

Figure 9 shows a tornado's thunderstorm as it might be seen from the ground. Such storms are large and powerful, drawing in warm, moist air at ground level from miles around. This storm is moving in a general left to right direction. The largest updraft is being pulled up through the cloud base below the main storm tower. This updraft can reach speeds of 100 to 200 mph (160 to 320 kmph) when it becomes the center of a full-fledged tornado. Strong winds are blowing from southwest to northeast. High in the cloud system the temperature drops, cooling the rising air and allowing the cloud to spread out; this forms an *anvil*, or flat-topped cloud.

Toward the bottom of the diagram, you can locate three important features: the *rain-free base*, the *wall cloud*, and the *precipitation area.* The rain-free base is a horizontal,

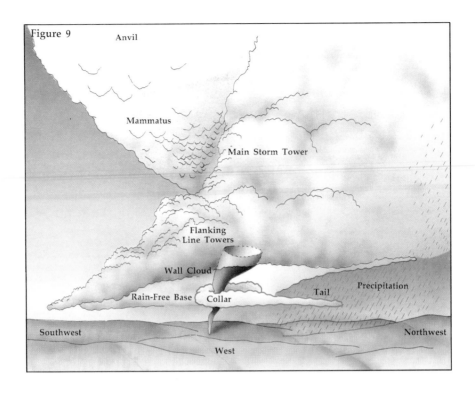

Figure 9

Anvil

Mammatus

Main Storm Tower

Flanking
Line Towers

Wall Cloud

Rain-Free Base   Collar   Tail   Precipitation

Southwest   Northwest

West

dark, cumulonimbus cloud base that has no *visible* precipitation beneath it. The rain-free base marks the location of the main updraft. Tornadoes can develop from: (1) wall clouds that are attached to the rain-free base or (2) from the rain-free base itself.

The wall cloud hangs lower than the rain-free base cloud. Its diameter is usually a quarter mile (.4 km), and this cloud is found below an intense updraft. Rotation can be observed in a wall cloud. This rotation may become intense enough to become a tornado.

The *precipitation shaft* is a visible column of rain or hail falling from a cloud base in the precipitation area. Above these shafts are powerful downdrafts, formed when the air in these storms has cooled. As long as great temperature differences between warm, rising air and cool, sinking air exist, the tornadic storm will continue.

Find the word *mammatus* on the diagram. Mammatus clouds (sometimes called *mamma clouds*) appear as hanging, rounded lumps or pouches under the surface of a cloud. They are formed by cooled air descending in the anvil of a thunderhead. These clouds do not produce tornadoes, hail, funnels, or any type of severe weather. However, they often accompany severe weather and are sometimes mistaken for a developing funnel.

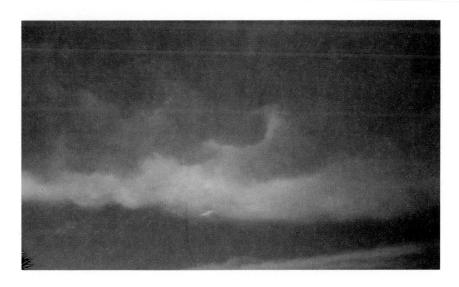

While mammatus clouds do not produce storms themselves, they often accompany severe weather.

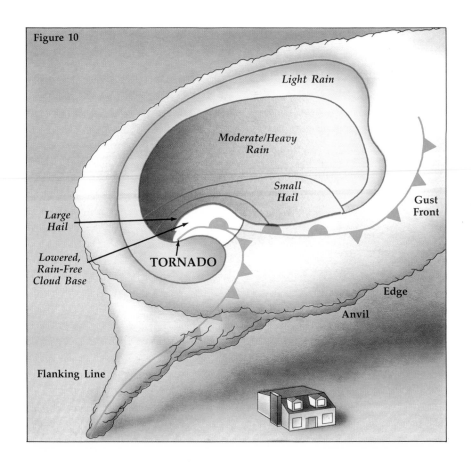

Figure 10

Light Rain

Moderate/Heavy Rain

Small Hail

Large Hail

Lowered, Rain-Free Cloud Base

TORNADO

Gust Front

Edge

Anvil

Flanking Line

The same storm diagrammed in Figure 9 is shown from above in Figure 10. This storm may continue for only a few minutes or for nearly an hour. Tornadoes of great strength rarely exist for longer periods. The famous Tri-State Tornado of 1925 swept through Missouri, Illinois, and Indiana, killing 689 people. It is reported to have lasted for several hours, a record that has never been equaled.

DEATH OF A TORNADO

As you have seen, it takes a lot of energy to "fuel" a tornado. This energy can be maintained for only short periods of time on land. Unlike its cousin the hurricane, which can churn and blister for weeks, the tornado runs out of energy quickly. Tornadoes get their energy from the thunderstorms that produce them. What makes a tornado run out of energy?

As the rains that accompany a tornado fall to the earth below, the earth is cooled. Soon, there is no longer enough heat energy to cause the air to rise. Without a steady supply of warm, moist, rising air, the thunderstorm weakens. As the storm weakens, its funnels thin out and rotate more slowly. Finally, the spinning stops. A few weak funnels may still form, but they lack the strength to do much damage. At this point, the damage is done, and cleanup must begin.

3

SCIENCE TAKES ON TORNADOES

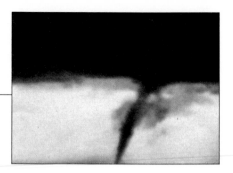

Considered by scientists and nonscientists alike to be nature's most violent storms, tornadoes have frightened human beings from earliest times. They have been difficult to study, and it was not until the settlement of North America that scientific research of tornadoes began in earnest.

North America suffers from a larger number of tornadoes than does any other continent except Australia. Since settlement of the western and midwestern sections of the United States took place mostly during the spring and summer months (tornado season), pioneers were often beset by "cyclones." These settlers had no warning of developing tornadoes and few defenses against them. Only the small population kept the number of deaths and injuries down.

Concern for warning the public about developing tornadoes began in 1870 when officers of the U.S. Army Signal Corps suggested that lives might be saved if people could take precautions against violent weather. Today, this branch of the U.S. Signal Corps has become the National Weather Service, and warning the public about possible weather problems is one of its chief duties.

THE NATIONAL WEATHER SERVICE

The National Weather Service (NWS) is a division of the U.S. Commerce Department's National Oceanic and Atmospheric Administration (NOAA). The NWS educates the public by printing pamphlets that are sent to civic organizations that request them. It also maintains over three hundred full-time weather stations that collect weather information. This information is then sent to the National Meteorological Center in Camp Springs, Maryland, where meteorologists predict the weather. From these predictions come tornado warnings as well as warnings of other severe weather.

To collect weather information used in the preparation of weather forecasts and storm warnings, the National Weather Service maintains weather stations throughout the country.

SPOTTERS

The NWS holds training sessions for tornado spotters, volunteer workers who relay information about tornadoes. The most reliable evidence that tornadoes have touched down in an area is still an eyewitness report. Spotters played an important part in warning residents of Wichita Falls, Texas, of an approaching tornado on April 10, 1979. Of the more than 18,000 people in the damage path of the tornado, only 44 were killed. Without warnings and the knowledge of safety rules, many more people certainly would have died.

Spotters have a dangerous job. They must leave shelter to look for evidence of tornadoes and then get the information to the NWS. People who act as tornado spotters do so to help save lives in the community.

CHASERS

Another group of people who try to find and observe tornadoes are known as *tornado chasers*. They chase tornadoes for the thrill of actually seeing nature's most powerful storm, but they are not careless amateurs. Tornado chasers know all about tornadoes and take precautions to protect themselves.

Tornado chasers are doctors, attorneys, auto mechanics, computer repairpeople, insurance brokers—anyone who has a deep interest in weather and the time to pursue the king of storms. But tornado chasers are not a bunch of foolhardy rowdies who hop into their trucks to race after killer storms. They use up-to-date equipment to track and photograph tornadoes. All the information they collect is turned over to weather scientists.

TOTO

Because the paths tornadoes follow are so unpredictable, it is nearly impossible to place instruments directly in their paths. But with the help of researchers at the National Severe Storms Laboratory in Norman, Oklahoma, scientists are able to collect more accurate information than ever before. By the early 1990s, people who live in tornado alley could routinely receive twenty minutes to an hour of warning about approaching storms.

The newest piece of equipment being used is called *TOTO* (Total Tornado Observatory). Tornado chasers drop TOTO, a 400-pound (182-kg) package of well-protected instruments, in the estimated path of a tornado to measure air pressure, air temperature, and wind speed. TOTO also takes photographs that can be analyzed to reveal even more about wind patterns within and around the funnel.

NEXRAD

The information gathered by TOTO helps meteorologists decide when to issue a tornado watch or warning. The information is analyzed and passed on through a series of rapid computer links. At the heart of this system is NEXRAD (Next Generation Radar), which replaced a twenty-five-year-old system too slow and too inaccurate to give up-to-the-minute warnings. Although it is estimated that NEXRAD will ultimately cost $1 billion and will take five years to completely install, it will pay for itself quickly in terms of better forecasts, fewer false warnings, and lives saved.

NEXRAD replaces the old WRS-57 radar. NEXRAD is radar of the Doppler type, which means it is able to detect

Left: A NEXRAD test tower houses a 28-foot (8.5-m) diameter radar antenna and electronics used to operate and monitor the system. The actual towers will be built of steel. Right: The NEXRAD antenna dish uses a pencil-thin beam to detect and measure precipitation, dust, or ice in the atmosphere. Scanning by the antenna will provide weather updates every five or six minutes.

motion in a cloud and also able to measure the size and intensity of a thunderstorm.

THE AIR FORCE
STUDIES TORNADOES

Another important aim in forecasting severe weather is increasing the safety of air traffic—civilian and military. The same wind shear forces responsible for helping a tornado form can pummel an airplane. Doppler radar may soon be installed in civilian airports throughout the country by the Federal Aviation Administration. It will almost certainly be installed even sooner at military bases.

Doppler Weather Radar is used in an airport traffic control tower to detect potentially severe thunderstorms over the airport.

Often, the U.S. Air Force tests new equipment before the NWS does. Although many military weather research projects are highly secret, some information is given to the public. Recently, flight tests of a tornado reconnaissance pod mounted on a USAF General Dynamics F-16/79 were made. The pod was mounted in the plane's nose and was controlled automatically. It recorded latitude, longitude, altitude, and velocity on each photo taken of the clouds it scanned. The camera in the pod had an infrared scanner so that it could operate in high haze and at night. In this way, the USAF was able to get extremely close to the spot within a cloud where tornadoes are usually born.

Many groups are working to understand tornadoes. They have saved thousands of lives by increasing warning time and uncovering the best defenses against these violent winds. But those responsible for using that warning time well and taking the final action to save lives are people like us. What we do with the information science gives us makes all the difference.

4.

MAKE YOURSELF TORNADO-WISE

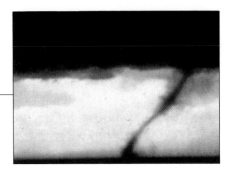

From the time you were a small child, parents and teachers have been warning you about the hazards of dangerous situations—don't go swimming alone, you might drown; don't play with matches, you might get burned; look both ways when you cross the street, or you might get hit by a car.

In the preceding chapters you read about the destructive forces of a tornado and the potential hazards of being caught in one. That is why it is important for you to know the safety rules and regulations. You can learn to protect yourself and others if you follow the correct procedures. Each year, the newspapers list hundreds of human casualties from tornadoes, but many of these lives could have been saved if the proper safety measures had been taken.

In 1898, when the U.S. Weather Bureau established its first meteorological station in the West Indies, it was a giant step forward in humankind's attempt to control the destructive power of nature. Winds can still not be controlled, but through the network of the National Weather Service and the Severe Storm Warning Center, adequate advance warnings of violent weather conditions can now be given.

TORNADO SIGNS

The combination of thunderstorms (thunder, lightning, and heavy winds), hail (large balls of ice), and a roaring noise (like a herd of stampeding elephants) are all signs of a possible tornado. If the possibility of a tornado exists, the National Weather Service issues a TORNADO WATCH; if a tornado has been sighted on the radar, it issues a TORNADO WARNING.

Each home, school, and community should have a tornado-preparedness plan. This plan should contain information for passing on watch and warning bulletins and specific details for action to be taken before and after a tornado strikes.

SCHOOL

In states that experience a high number of tornadoes each year, all schools are now required to conduct periodic drills and have a plan of action in the event of a storm. Each room in your school should display a sign that tells you where to go and what to do during a tornado drill.

During a drill, follow the instructions of your teacher. Ask for information if the teacher doesn't volunteer it. Stay away from rooms with wide roofs that could collapse easily, such as gymnasiums and auditoriums. Go to an inside wall on the lowest floor, kneel on the floor facing the wall, and put your hands over your head. Keep calm and help anyone who might be frightened.

HOME

If you are home alone in a severe thunderstorm and you hear hail or a roaring noise—or you see a dark funnel: (1) Turn on your television or radio to find out if a tornado has

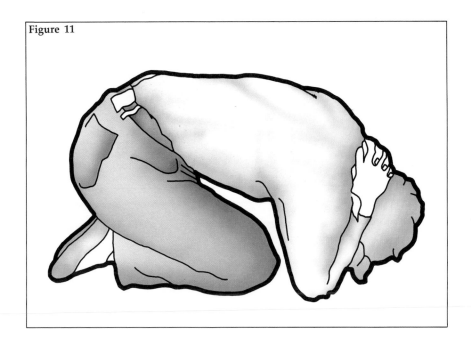

Figure 11

been spotted. All television stations project tornado watch or tornado warning signs on the screen. (2) Go to the basement and get under the stairs or a piece of heavy furniture. (3) If you have no basement, get in a closet in the middle of the house. (4) If you live in a mobile home, get out. Go to a public shelter or to a neighbor's basement.

Disaster supplies (flashlight, transistor radio, candles, matches, etc.) should be kept in your home at all times. When a tornado is spotted, avoid using the telephone, because it is a conductor of electricity.

If advance warning is given of a possible interruption in the water supply, store water in clean, covered containers or in the bathtub.

With advance planning, you will know the best places in your home to find shelter in case of a tornado.

OUTSIDE

If you are in a store or shopping mall when a tornado strikes, people who work there will tell you the safest place to go. If you are in a car, get out; if you can't reach a shelter or building, lie flat in a ditch or crouch next to a building, covering your head with your hands.

Many times tornadoes are accompanied by lightning, which is also dangerous. Don't touch any metal objects such as bicycles or wire fences, and stay clear of tall trees and open water.

There is a lot of information about tornadoes and tornado safety available to you. Many states sound sirens when a tornado has been spotted, skits are staged in schools to show students the dangers of twisters, and tornado safety week is observed to reinforce the information presented.

You, as an individual, can make a difference. Observe all rules and behave responsibly when you have tornado drills. You could someday save your own life or that of a classmate.

TORNADO MYTHS AND REALITIES

The difference between reality and myth could be the difference between life and death in an emergency. Planning and knowledge of safety procedures are very important when reaction time is measured in seconds, such as with severe storms and tornadoes. History has shown that many tornado deaths result from improper action rather than a lack of advance warning. The Ohio Committee on Tornado Safety is working to increase safety awareness, and one way to do that is to dispel rumors and expose fiction.*

Myth: The safest place in a home or building is the southwest corner.

Reality: A storm cellar or basement is best, but if neither is available, a small windowless room or closet in the center

Tornado Myths and Realities courtesy of the Ohio Disaster Services Agency, 2825 West Granville Road, Worthington, Ohio 43085

of the home offers the best protection. External walls should be avoided. Most damage occurs on the windward side of a structure.

Myth: Windows should be opened to reduce damage from the tornado's drop in atmospheric pressure.

Reality: Most residences and commercial buildings have enough natural venting to relieve any change in atmospheric pressure as a result of tornadoes. By taking the time to open windows, you are exposing yourself to added dan-

The strong winds of a tornado can destroy buildings, uproot trees, and send dangerous debris flying into the air.

ger from flying glass and debris. In addition, you may expose the inside of your home to water damage from storms that may accompany tornadoes.

Myth: When a tornado approaches, it is best to flee in your automobile.

Reality: A tornado's direction and speed of travel may be erratic, and your escape route could become blocked. Tornadoes travel at speeds as high as 70 mph (112 kmph). Wind-blown debris may approach speeds near 300 mph (480 kmph). In most cases, it is best to leave your car and take cover in a sturdy home or building. If a shelter is not available, move as far as possible from your car and lie flat in a low spot and cover your head.

Myth: A mobile home is a safe place to be if it is tied down.

Reality: All occupants of mobile homes, with or without tie-downs, should evacuate to more substantial structures or shelter anytime a severe thunderstorm or tornado threatens. Tie-downs are designed to reduce damage and injuries that occur from a mobile home sliding or overturning. While tie-downs can reduce damage, they do not provide the personal protection needed against tornado winds and debris, which may reach speeds of 100 to 300 mph (160 to 480 kmph).

5

SCIENCE PROJECTS AND RELATED ACTIVITIES

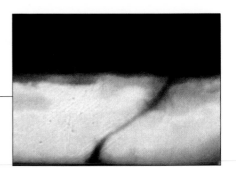

This section offers ideas for science projects and other school activities related to tornadoes. You might wish to use these for a school science project or do them just for fun.

The Force of the Wind. The wind velocity in a tornado is great enough to drive blades of grass or straws through the trunks of trees. It sounds incredible! To prove it can be done, you will need a potato and a plastic drinking straw.

Place the end of the drinking straw against the potato and push as hard as you can. What happens? Did the straw bend or break? Why?

Now hold a straw at least 2 feet (.6 m) from the potato and thrust it into the potato as hard as you can. What happened? Did the straw go into the potato? Why?

The greater the velocity of matter, the greater its momentum. The faster you make the straw move, the greater its force when it strikes the potato and the deeper it will penetrate.

Pressure. We rarely notice that we live at the bottom of a deep sea of air that presses down on us with great force.

We run and jump against the air without feeling its weight at all. But air pressure is a powerful force, especially in the vortex of a tornado. Here are some activities that will show you the strength of the air around you.

Crush the Jug. You will need a gallon-size plastic milk jug, a plastic or rubber hose of the type used with a spray attachment in the bathtub, and water.

Stretch the end of the hose over the mouth of the plastic jug and fill the jug with water. This drives out the air. Hold the free end of the hose over a sink or bucket and turn the jug upside down (see Figure 12). As the water leaves the jug, the pressure inside will drop. Normal air pressure that feels comfortable to you will press inward, crushing the jug.

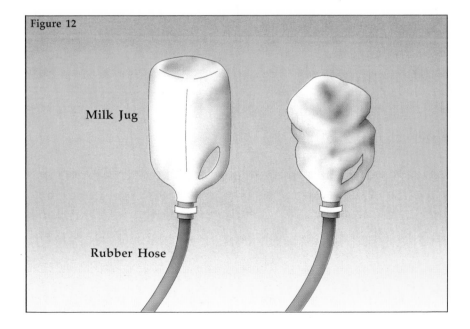

Figure 12

Milk Jug

Rubber Hose

Crush the Can. For this experiment, you should have adult supervision. You will need a one-gallon metal can such as the type used to store gasoline or duplicating fluid. You will also need a heat source such as a hot plate. Ice is optional.

Thoroughly wash the inside of the can to clean out any flammable liquid. Place water in the bottom of the can to a depth of about 2 inches (5 cm). With the cap off, heat the can on the hot plate or Bunsen burner until the water boils and steam can be seen coming from the can. Remove the can from the heat and cap it as tightly as possible.

You can allow the can to cool slowly at room temperature or place it in a bucket of ice. As the can cools, the steam inside condenses and takes up less room. This causes the pressure inside the can to drop (just as it does in the eye of a tornado). Since there is less pressure inside the can, the air outside can press inward with enough force to crush the can.

The following activities will give you a chance to create small tornadoes and will illustrate the rotation that occurs in a vortex.

Liquid Tornado. Fill a mayonnaise or mason jar with water. Make the water swirl by stirring it with a spoon or stirring rod. Drop in a few drops of food coloring or ink. What happens to the color?

Another way to make a tornado in a bottle is to mix water, food coloring, and a few drops of liquid soap in a quart jar. Tightly cap the jar. Give the jar a quick twist with both hands and watch the vortex appear in the jar.

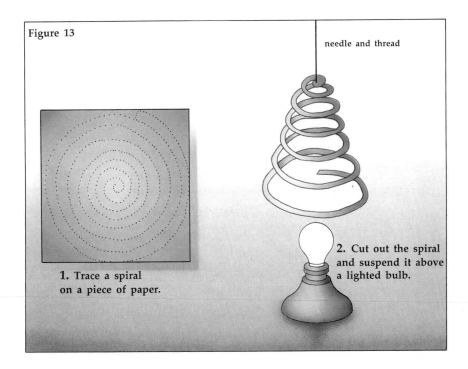

Figure 13

needle and thread

1. Trace a spiral on a piece of paper.

2. Cut out the spiral and suspend it above a lighted bulb.

Dust Devils. Dust devils are the smallest of twisters, but their cause is the same as that of the devastating tornadoes. To make a dust devil, trace a spiral on a piece of paper. Cut out the spiral. Using a threaded needle, suspend the spiral above a lighted light bulb, as shown in Figure 13.

Warm air rising from the heat source causes the spiral to turn. In a similar way, heat from the warm earth causes air to rise (especially in the summer). As the air moves upward, cooler air moves toward the rising mass to take its place and upsets the balance of air pressure. The warm air then begins to whirl around a low-pressure center. As the air rises, it carries dust up with it.

Larger Tornado. You can make a more powerful tornado by directing warm, moist air upward within a rectangular box. For this activity, you will need:

a pan of water

an electric hot plate

two 12- × 30-inch (30 × 76-cm) panes of glass

two 12- × 30-inch (30 × 76-cm) plywood panels

a cardboard tube 4 feet (122 cm) long

and 6 inches (15 cm) in diameter

wood to construct a frame, as shown at right

Place the panels of glass and plywood in such a way as to allow a 1-inch opening at each corner for air to enter and circulate in a counterclockwise direction (see Figure 14). Cut a 6-inch hole in the center of the box's top, and place the cardboard tube over it to make an updraft. The hot plate should be placed in the center of the box with a pan of boiling water on it. If a light is directed through one of the glass panels and viewed through the other, the vortex is more easily seen.

Charting Tornadoes. During tornado season, you can clip newspaper articles about tornadoes and listen to the weather reports on the radio and television. Draw a map of the United States, then read newspapers and listen to weather reports. Mark on your map where tornadoes have been spotted, where warnings have been issued, and where tornadoes have touched down. Many public agencies will send information to you free of charge if you write to them.

Field Trips. Your teacher might be interested in taking your class to various museums that specialize in displays of sci-

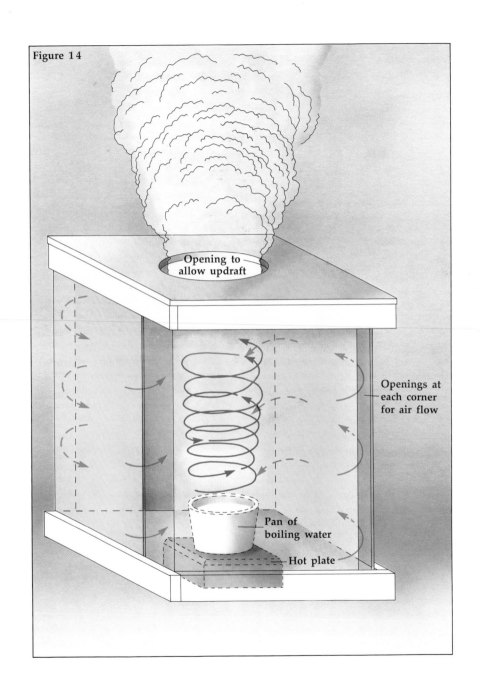

Figure 14

Opening to allow updraft

Openings at each corner for air flow

Pan of boiling water

Hot plate

Meteorologists for the National Weather Service collect data to be used in the development of weather forecasts.

ence and technology. Other possibilities for field trips would be a visit to a weather station, an interview with a meteorologist (a person who studies the weather), or a trip to the weather department of a college or university.

Science Reports. When your science teacher assigns a report, you might be interested in choosing one of the following topics, all of which are related to tornadoes:

    Air pressure
    Coriolis effect
    Fujita-Pearson scale

NEXRAD (Next Generation Radar)

NOAA (National Oceanic and Atmospheric Administration)

Skywarn

Spotters

Tornado Alley

TOTO (Total Tornado Observatory)

Tri-State Tornado

You might also explore the careers of people who make their living in weather-related areas. Find out what it takes to be a meteorologist (physical or operational), a climatologist, or a weather forecaster. Examine the workplace and the daily responsibilities of the people who have these jobs.

Book Reports. In recent years, there has been an increase in tornado awareness. Some excellent stories have been written that describe the heroism displayed by people caught in the path of a destructive storm. For information and enjoyment, try reading:

Milton, Hilary. *Tornado.* New York: Franklin Watts, 1983.

Ruckman, Ivy. *Night of the Twisters.* New York: Harper & Row, 1984.

Shore, June. *Summer Storm.* Nashville: Abington Press, 1977.

BIBLIOGRAPHY

Books
Baum, Frank. *The Wizard of Oz.* New York: Macmillan, 1962.
Eagleman, Joe R. *Severe & Unusual Weather.* New York: Van Nostrand Reinholdt Co., 1983.
Gibilsco, Stan. *Violent Weather: Hurricanes, Tornadoes & Storms.* Blue Summit Ridge, PA: Tab Books, Inc., 1984.
Guinness Book of Weather. Guinness Superlatives. Great Britain, 1977.
Kals, W. S. *The Riddle of the Winds.* New York: Doubleday, 1977.
Winchester, James. *Hurricanes, Storms, Tornadoes.* New York: G. P. Putnam's Sons, 1968.

Magazine Articles
Clary, Mike. "Tornado Chasing." *Weatherwise.* June 1986, pp. 137–145.
Miller, Pete. "Tornado." *National Geographic.* June 1987, pp. 689–714.
Milner, Samuel. "NEXRAD." *Weatherwise.* April 1986, pp. 72–85.
Snow, John T. "The Tornado." *Scientific American.* April 1984, pp. 86–96.
Teitelman, Robert. "The Eyes of NEXRAD." *Forbes.* March 26, 1984, pp. 202–208.
Vonnegut, Bernard. "Inside the Tornado." *Natural History.* April 1968, pp. 26–32.

We have also used pamphlets from the following organizations:
Ohio Insurance Institute, P.O. Box 632, Columbus, OH 43216
National Oceanic and Atmospheric Administration, Rockville, MD 20852
National Severe Storms Laboratory, 1313 Halley Circle, Norman, OK 73060.

INDEX